SAFARI READERS
3
BOOK STAGE

Lions

SAFARI
READERS

Tristan Walters

For Billy & Phoebe

- the original Safari Readers!

Copyright © 2019 Safari Readers

www.safarireaders.com

Written & Designed by Tristan Walters

Abbreviations - FreeVectorMaps (FVM); Shutterstock (SS). Cover (background). Olesya Zadorozhnaya/SS; Cover (middle), Sergei Mironenko/SS; 1. Maggy Mayer/SS; 2-3, Simon Eeman/SS; 4, Andrew Paul Deer/SS; 5, Rhoeo/SS; 6-7 (background), Andrzej Kubik/SS; 6, Mikhail Kolesnikov/SS; 7, Michael Wick/SS; 8, Chad Littlejohn/SS; 9, Ondrej Prosicky/SS; 10, MPH Photos/SS; 11, FreeVectorMaps/FVM; 11, Kshitij30/SS; 12, Riaan van den Berg/SS; 13 (top left), Brina L Bunt SS; 13 (top right), Debbie Steinhausser/SS; 13 (bottom left), Riaan van den Berg/SS; 13 (bottom right), Thomas Retterath/SS; 14, Tobie Oosthuizen/SS; 16-1 Gudkov Andrey/SS; 17 (1st/4th), Gudkov Andrey/SS; 17 (2nd), NaniP/SS; 17 (3rd), Wolfgang Franz/SS; 18, Mogens Trolle/SS; 19 (1st), Tobie Osthuizen/SS; 19 (2nd Graham Needham/SS; 19 (3rd/4th), Rostislav Stach/SS; 20, Julian W/SS; 21 (top left), Maggy Meyer/SS; 21 (bottom right), Keith Jenkinson/SS; 21 (bottom left Theodore Mattas/SS; 21 (top right), Erwin Niemand/SS; 22, Brina L Bunt/SS; 23, PhotocechCZ/SS; 24, Rudi van der Heever/SS; 25, natchapohn/SS; 26, Mar Turcan/SS; 28, Sergey Novikov/SS; Back (background), Olesya Zadorozhnaya/SS. Animation Images (back, 5, 7, 9, 11, 23-28), Memo Angeles/SS.

Contents

What is a lion?

Did you know?
The roar of a lion can be heard from over 8km away!

Lions are a **mammal** that belong to the cat family. They are the second largest of the big cats and one of the few that can roar.

Do you know your family tree?

LION FAMILY TREE

PANTHERA

snow leopard

tiger

leopard

jaguar

lion

Check out the words in **bold** in our glossary on the back page.

real size

Did you know?
A lion's tooth can be up to 7cm long!

LION

SCIENTIFIC NAME
Panthera leo

SIZE
Up to 2.5m long

WEIGHT
Up to 225 kg

SPEED
70 km per hour

AGE
Up to 20 years

balancing when running

long tail

sharp claws

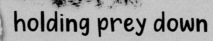

holding prey down

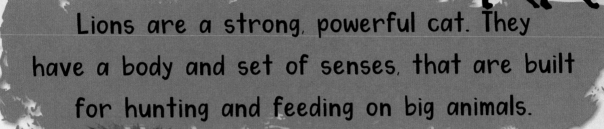

Lions are a strong, powerful cat. They have a body and set of senses, that are built for hunting and feeding on big animals.

pointed teeth

biting and killing prey

Can you read and match each label on the lion?

rough tongue

scraping meat off of bones

What do lions look like?

Did you know?
A lion's mane turns darker as it gets older.

Female Lion

Male Lion

Can you spot any differences?

Not all lions look the same. Male lions are a lot bigger than females. Males also have a band of hair around their neck called a mane.

9

Where do lions live?

Did you know?
A lion's fur helps them to keep camouflaged in the long grass.

North America

Europe

Asia

Africa

South America

Oceania

African Lion
Asiatic Lion

N

Which continent do you live in?

Asiatic Lion

Asiatic lions have smaller manes than than African lions.

Lions live in grasslands, thick bush and desert across parts of Africa. There is still one group of lions that lives in a forest in Asia.

How many lions live in a pride?

Did you know?
Lions are the only kind of cat that live in groups.

Lions live together in a large group called a pride. Most lion prides include up to three males, a dozen females and their young cubs.

LION PRIDE FACTS

Lions in a pride will sleep for 20 hours a day!

zzzZZZ

Some lions climb trees to avoid flies and biting insects.

Some 'super prides' have up to 40 lions!

Lions in a pride bond with each other by rubbing heads, licking and purring.

How big is a lion's territory?

Did you know?
Invading male lions often kill any old males or cubs in the pride.

Each pride has its own land, called a **territory**. The male lion defends the pride's land and fights any other lions that come too close.

LION TERRITORY

TEAMWORK
Some male lions team up with family members to lead a pride.

⚠ WARNING ⚠
Lions roar and scent mark to warn other lions to stay away.

SIZE MATTERS
A lion's territory can be up to 300km^2 – that's the same size as some cities!

What do lions eat?

Lions are **carnivores**. They hunt and feed on lots of different big animals, such as gazelle, zebra, buffalo, giraffe and even elephant!

wildebeest

giraffe

gazelle

zebra

How do lions hunt?

Lionesses do most of the hunting in a pride. The lions hunt together as a team so they can catch prey much bigger than themselves.

HOW LIONS HUNT

Most lion hunts are at dusk or dawn.

1 THE STALK

Lions sneak up and get as close to their prey as they can without being seen.

THE CHASE 2

Lions will often attack as a group. They chase their prey and try and knock it to the ground.

3 THE KILL

The lead lioness will often make the kill with a bite to the neck. Only 20% of hunts end in a kill!

THE FEAST 4

Lions eat up to 20kg at a time! They will often go another week without a meal.

WARNING!
HORNS HURT LIONS!

How many cubs are in a litter?

Did you know?
Lion cubs have spots to give them extra **camouflage**.

Suckling. Cubs will drink their mother's milk for up to ten months.

Growing. Cubs grow quickly and are ready to hunt after a year.

Play Fighting. Cubs learn vital hunting skills when play fighting.

Hiding. Lots of animals will kill lion cubs if they find them.

Lions have up to six cubs in a **litter**. The lioness hides her cubs in a den for the first six weeks, away from other animals.

Why are lions in trouble?

LION POPULATION
~~50,000~~
25,000

Did you know?
The number of lions
has halved in just 20 years!

CONSERVATION STATUS

Only 500 Asiatic lions are left in the wild!

Where lions live

Where lions used to live

What will happen to the number of lions if this carries on?

The number of lions is falling quickly. Many lions are killed for sport or shot by farmers for coming too close to their land and animals.

Lion Puzzle

Can you match the animal with its food?

lion

gazelle

aardvark

meerkat

Safari Readers

The 'Safari Readers' books are specially designed to help children learn to read. Based on leading teaching practice, this series enables children to develop a range of reading skills and create a love of reading and language through wild and exciting topics.

Enjoy the ride!

Reading is fun! These books are best enjoyed when reading together.

The child may need some help reading the smaller text.

The larger text is for the child to read.

There is a book for all our 'Safari Readers' out there.

Why not join 'Safari Sam' and 'Safari Suzy' and explore the other books

we have in the series!

STAGE 1

Cheetahs Flamingos Wolves Giraffes Dolphins

☐ ☐ ☐ ☐ ☐

STAGE 2

Sea Turtles Tigers Elephants Polar Bears Gorillas

☐ ☐ ☐ ☐ ☐

STAGE 3

Sharks Lions Penguins Snakes Monkeys

☐ ✓ ☐ ☐ ☐

For more information check out our website:

WWW.SAFARIREADERS.COM

Glossary

Can you remember all of the new words we have learnt?

Mammal an animal that feeds its young milk and (in most cases) has hair or fur.

Camouflage a pattern on an animal's skin or coat that helps it hide in the place it lives.

Territory an area of land that an animal or group lives in that is protected from others.

Carnivore an animal that only eats meat.

Litter a group of young animals born at the same time.